The Meter is Irregular

Volume 2

Unleashing Teenage Werewolves

Roddy

1st WORLD
PUBLISHING

The Meter is Irregular, Volume 2

Roddy

Copyright © 2014 Rodney Charles

Published by 1st World Publishing
P.O. Box 2211, Fairfield, Iowa 52556
tel: 641-209-5000 • fax: 866-440-5234
web: www.1stworldpublishing.com

First Edition

LCCN: 2014937134
ISBN: 978-1-4218-8685-5

Acknowledgments

We cannot be without the Grand-Wolves of the pack
Gertrud, Karl, Raj and Ravi

Dedication

To those I frighten
Accept my apology and confession

To my natural enemies
Your gifts are valued most of all

I hunt with the pack
And my loyalty is practice

Preface

I admit honestly
I know nothing concerning poetry
But I do know my own bodily appetites
I'm an expert on that

If you are too
Hum along with me
I'll croon you a story
And you sing one for me

A note on style:

My imperfections are deliberate
I'm apt to rush
Eager to capture a moment

After all
I wrote these poems for my children
And sunlight doesn't wait to hear my voice

There is only one
I hope to impress
And she already loves me
Despite protestation

CONTENTS

Upstate New York

The sun shone through me today
Leaving me unable to know
What was sun
And what was not

Flooded with memories
Of so many New York mornings
When you opened me
Urging me to look
And see who's there

At first
You frightened me
Your warm touch
Consumed my every notion

I don't know how many days
I wandered like a madman
Drunk with permanent addiction
Drinking only your daylight

But fear of loss
Loss of ego
Caused me to throw myself hard upon the wall
Begging for sobriety

What kind of fool
Throws sunlight out of his house
Demanding dark ignorance
And spiritual starvation

For twenty years you kept knocking
Faithfully waiting
Hoping I would open a window
And look to see you there

This is how you taught me love, eventually
By consuming my littleness
And letting the current take me

Fast

The emptiness in my mind
Allows me to heed
The humming of my soul
Your soul

I often leave my belly empty
For days, sometimes weeks
To empty my mind
And dance
To the deep low frequency
That drowns even Gabriel's trumpet

Days of liberated drunkenness
Liquid oxygen
Forcing youth and energy
Into consecrated limbs
Tempting hygiene
And the promise of
Unpolluted humility

Overfed
My mind distends
With secret messages
Undigested urges
And unadorned twaddle

Why do we endure this supersized thoughtlessness?

Mothers and physicians
Offer sound remedies
Rendered ineffectual
By unwashed bowels
And swollen, faded vessels

Acidic inequity
Breeds fog, violence
And psychological disturbance
Cured readily through fasting
A poet's silence
Or urgent nuclear all-out drug assaults

The best medicine
Is habitual vacuity
Pure water and good company
Addictive
Like mother's milk
And selfless love

Katrina

Today I breathed the impossible
All over again
The same wind that gunned down Orleans
Kissed my face
Calming sweat from my brow

The lordly wind
Spoke of love and mercy
Turning over the sky
Inhaling and exhaling
Annihilation

A balance unwritten
By never-ending death

Understood by souls
Made whole
In the course of unification

All the same
She brings tears
Of loss and joy
The same wind
The storm of me

Sobriety

Fashionistas say God is dead
I say
Pour this man
Another round
He is far too sober
To understand addiction

Sales and service
Are bullish
Profits reaped by holy investors

But homeless pundits
Take no notice of wooly doctrines

Too much wine
Cures any dogma
Pure gold poured into fragile clay pots
Knowing nothing whatsoever
But existence and bearing

Charms

Rings and gems
Fall from my carcass
Like autumn leaves

But I wear a garland of priceless jumble
Collections of scars and sweet mysteries
From unknown years of roaming and hygiene

No food cures hunger
Born of hushed deprivation

A nursing infant
Craves only mothers' milk

Sleep Breath

August Iowa
Twilight crickets rev their engines
Racing to mate
Expecting a hit

Like desert fathers
Muttering mantras for centuries
I feel the rhythm of your rubbing
In step with my snoring remains

Just another trance
Like children searching
For sex and war
Worth only dream gold

Don't be satisfied
With the gist of poetry
Discern the breathing
Of the artist

Death

Some people say
Death is dust
What a hangover
Death gives me

Where is this
Invisible ocean of blackness
Hiding plainly
In the dread of self-discovery?

Owning everything
The emperor of the stars
Still cries for lost habits
With fearful unfamiliarity for emptiness

You see why
I get this hangover?

Self imprisonment
And the absence of bodily patience
Lead me to drink with others
Weaned of fear and alteration

When this mysterious garment
Grows heavy and cold with age
I'll blend its sweet shadow
With never-ending death
Like ginger tea and honey

Three-Ringed Circus

Don't be afraid
When all the hidden things
Come to life

They come to life
As proof of grace

We may never know the origin of our lesions
We can't know all we've done
But God is not offended by ill-bred mutilation
With no trouble she dissolves revulsion

Secrecy is a lie
Conceived in fear

When we injure
We draw injury to ourselves

But this echo ends mute
With an act of mercy

Jesus knew this
Better than anyone
The kernel of true manhood

Sacred Ground

You appear in my terrace
Selling the gospel of enthusiasm
Eager to multiply your security
With votes and participation

Stopping the words
I inhale their meaning

And like ancient scriptures
They rust and turn to stone

In mystic light
Each breath
Spawns ecstasy
Contorting my twisted neck
With apparition and splendor

Will you understand
When I kneel to you now?

Involuntarily I am surrendered
By a million customs to kiss the ground

Are you fearful of this madness?
Once I was
But it passed in an instance of breathless passion
Leaving me
Beyond comprehension
Lips to the ground

Odd Lockdown

The divinity of science
Imprisons herself
In ignorance
By hiding the key
To break out

Fear Face

Primal
Weaponless
Resisting shadows
Putrid graveyard of torment
I oppose you

Your belief
Is you

Lurid nightmare
Satan's guardian
A jamboree of headless hosts
Shitting blood

F%#k you
You'll perish
In this butcher's stream
Of mucus and rot

Your belief
Is you

Willingly, I sink my arm
Inside the serpent's throat

Clarity
Naked weakness
Rupture exposed
All human suffering ceased

Effusive alive

Uncertain
Unwilling
You evaporate

Do I fear you still?
No
Fear is my own creation

Ask Directions

Fairfield is filled with drunkards
Wandering aimlessly at 4:00 AM

Not knowing they're drunk
They cannot find their way home

Taverns, by no means, shut their doors
Brewing unique and current blends

My drunken soul is not homeless
It originated somewhere

Knowing this
I may soon be sober.

This drunkenness
Is awkward
But I've stumbled this far
Surely these verses will lug me home

Ordinary Sensitivity

Allow gravity
To pull you to your goddess
Who'll crib you
Like an undiscovered pearl

Spinning like a child
You'll shout "the ground is turning"
But pearls yearn discovery
And vertigo passes, once bearing is poised

Allow faithful gravity

A chicken will not mate with a turtle
Predictably, each living creature
Trusts instinct
For sustenance and love

Evident

Remind me again
How I ruined the life you hoped to enclose

No mother, no father, buried in woe
Thrown from your nest, unable to fly

Ignored

Is a wolf hidden among the sheep?
Who bears a prison where no margins exist?

Disregarded

The sun will grow cold
From your longing for warmth

So drink honest wine
Your goddess is near

But unnoticed

Fountainheads

Sleep erases mainly my memories
But not my thoughts

Rambling alongside I understand
What alters dreams
But what would be the value of that?

Holy wine is intoxicating
Until the bottle's dry

Ecstasy annihilates decency
And children mock drunkards
Tricking them with their games

If you cannot linger any longer
Find a partner
Brewing ambrosia
From a fountain
Near home

Noisy Asses

Tears
Are poetry
Fluent
With poise
In all accents

Like cherished Tea
Luring
Addicts of
Custom
To drunkenness

Like fools
Recovery
Is fixation
Instituted
By blind madmen

Fright
May stunt youth
But tears
Will drown you
In due course

Origins

Life began as medicine
Primordial milk
And grew into lunacy
A new remedy for pain

Still, the beautiful
Adore the sordid mysteries
Flattering mutual charity
And sacred imperfection

Life is not mere aestheticism
It is hygiene
Enforcing cleanliness
For celestial votaries
Entering
The abode of the humble
Free
Of personal drama

What to Fear Most

Habitual helplessness
Fear
Denial
Reminiscent of waves
Washing shipwrecked fish

A Fool and His Chai

Friday the 13th (12-13-13)

The bottomless harmony of words
Overwhelms me
With wild cellular alteration
Streamlining DNA

Sob bursting
Shivering effervescent
Abandonment
Not possible to care
How foolish I appear

It's not the words
But the light
And hum
Beneath the breath of me

Puffing
Unburdened by cessation
Inundated with memories
Of mother's lips on infant plump

Transcendent goddess
Your gifts overwhelm me
Howling past love

Trembling willingly
Impossible to care
For coffeehouse onlookers
Whose troubled eyes
Jog my sanity
In time to mop costly tears
From laptop keys

Praise you beloved rapture
For assembling this fool
This fictitious shadow
Hinting of supernatural clarity

Immeasurable blaze
Quake me to bits
I can only howl
With natural communion

False Memory

Accept love
Unaltered
Dependant on nothing
Unrequited

Memory

Resembling freedom

Is a fragile thing

Confidence
Akin to memory
Is fiction

Bitter
I am bitterness

Passionate
My bones are enlightened

Empty
I am fullness

Afflicted
I feel the need to laugh

Judged
I am condemnatory

Lacking empathy
We are poor

Excuse my wandering
But do you know
How hard it is to feign normalcy
When organization is absurd?

Aren't we all searching for Popeye?

Blueblood

Thankfully
We can never be separated
From the Ass
That carries us

Sunrise reminds me
Of faithful love
The full moon
At all times, reminds me of you

Looking up at the stars
Blown away again
I am blessed
With a right royal Ass

Communiqué

Damp saline verse
Or tears of joy

Empathy is an accent

Without invention

Nudge

My mind repeatedly breaks
For three days
With moon waxing

Sleepless
I roam yesterday's avenues
And dream of snoring

Why this distraction?
A reminder
Of infancy

And who rules gravity
The oceans
And me

United

Words are echoes
From a bit of Spirit
Unreachable
Through sound reason

Oceanic ruin
Effervescent madness
And felonious hums
Offer sweet sobriety and zeal
For social giddiness

But torn shoes
And my worn bike tires
Help me remember
The equivalent worth of original clay

Lost and Found

Some nights
I sleep like granite

Passing hours of erosion
Awake, remembering nothing

I live backwards
Ignorant of my addiction
To infatuated senses

Are you sure
I can't shed this compulsion
With cerebral force and austerity?

Yes
Exhaustion defeats me

And falling
You cradle me in grace

Again, again
And again

Debt Ceiling October 2013

The angst-armies
And politicians
Fought on CNN again last night

Driving me to
Occupied abstraction

Dissonant notes
On trumpets and strings
Dissolving
To pulse
And
Energetic hum

All this fantasy
Shows me the ocean again
So I'm blessed
By Breaking News

And increased or decreased taxes

Weapons

An infant
Cannot discern
The symbols of life
The changing seasons
Urging us to transform
Devoid of fright and failure

Like petty thieves
Dogmas, selfish for power
Sell absolutions
Dividing kith and kin
With fear and loss

Violent weapons
Aimed
At your soul
Megatons of control
Capable of decisive sacred annihilation

An infant
Cannot discern
The changing seasons

Earth and Water

Atheists
With their religious doctrines
Appear in my tea room
Preaching the gospel
Of sex
Indigestion
And dust

For non-God's sake
Have another drink
Your mad evangelism
Has made you limp and impotent
Junk in hand
Spewing seed
Like a well gone dry

Put down your pamphlet
Go to your temple
I'll go to mine

I have tea to drink now
You're welcome to join
But I'd appreciate you
Putting your inadequacies
Back in your pants

It is really
Very ill-mannered

Breaking the Bottle

You told me the knower's of authenticity
Are likewise surprised
By original glimmers of mystical stirring

It's not possible to anticipate
Cataclysmic adoration
Without shattering sanity

No wonder saints and madmen
Are indistinguishable

How does this cosmos pass
Lock stock and barrel
Through the eye of a needle?

I am so pleased with you

Comparative

Religion
Great faith
And celebrity mystics consent
The soul lives
In breath suspended

The grandeur
Of little things
And the littleness
Of great things
Are here balanced

One
Singular miracle
Shines full overhead
Diminishing shadows
In passionate breathlessness

Every story told
Dreamt itself
Each written word
Loses the richness
Of emptiness

But the dream continues
Symbols and shadows
Worthy of faith
As the soul lives
In the silence of breath

Palindrome

Emancipate crude idealism
With ginger fresh tea

The apostle of tea was born
Promoting universal mirrors

Gleaning the tea-service
The poet offers empathy
Celebrating the code of tea
As God

Tea plants gathering curled leaves
Plucked by morning light
Emancipate crude idealism

Chimera

Every written word
Adds shadows
To morning light

How did I ever learn to read?

Every soul's deathbed
Pregnant with self-honesty
Is conclusively alive

How did I ever learn to fear?

Even the trivial and wrong
Hint of original conception
Gathers rust or gold

How did I ever learn to judge?

My mother taught me
"When ghosts appear in dreams
Run straight at them."
They will cease

And you will know what is real

Courage

A bud is shy
But motherhood presses
Courageous infants
Pregnant with purpose
To bloom seductive

A rhythm
Without resistance
Elemental jazz
An intercourse
Of time, space and spirit

Don't bother
Defining death
Unaware of itself
It falls into place
Obedient to our will

Water Turns

Poems hurl themselves
Upon the shore
Uncovering treasure
Beneath the sand

Wave upon wave
Graceful passages
Caught in sea foam
Link both worlds

The ocean
And everything born of it

Vote

Drowned again
With CNN
What is this fascination with terms?
Notes, executed to summon
Musical diversion and lyric

Kettle drums beating
Confidence into
Self-delusion

Brass blowhards
Broadcasting amnesia

Flute and strings
Humming below
Hissing information
Devoid of choir
Or art

Evening news
Grovels awe
Leavening
Political hush
And silent rhythm

Being independent
I vote
For the whirlwind
In my gut

Led by Thoreau

Lessons From Congo

Consider fear and nakedness

Paralyzed survival
Morning endurance
Waking devastation
Forgotten values
Judgment and blame
Self-amnesia
Unanswered love

Don't go back to sleep

Rally in the meadow
Where springs
Are so abundant with secrets
We are mute
Endowed with new ears
Keen for the color and detail of drama

Where poem and poet change places

Your Own Myth

Although male
I am a woman in labor
Pregnant with mystery
Contracting with curiosity

I will not abort motherhood
Being royally flanked
My child is a poet, like you
A pearl in a clam shell

Bull Shh Meter

Some days
I smell my own decay
That's when I know
I've overeaten

This stench of deficiency
Has once again
Distracted me
With a woodpile of duties

But I love the laughter
That comes
Soon after I ask
Why I dance around the obvious truth

Playing Field

Do you worry about things going badly?
Be suspicious
It may be bait
For popularity

Your soul knows
How to shape verse
Your customers will applaud
Or chew quietly

Either way
Children will whoop in the fields
With mirth and prayers
Of perfect pitch
With or without audience

And you have yourself to thank

Non-Alcoholic

You spoke to me on Facebook
Dictating the "rules of love"
Unconscious and insane
You asked me to follow you

People tell me you are a drunk
But I think you aren't drunk enough
The desert is shifting in your heart
Howling for hallowed plum

Like me
Your thirst is addiction
But the dark suggestions you cling to
Keep you self-dead and sober, like a dirty joke.

Tomorrow
You'll wake up drunk
Craving consecrated wine
And the rules of love
Won't matter anymore

Propaganda

Where is that tonic
Given only to those
Too wounded to hope

I need more grace than I ever imagined

Tangled in knots
What is this assembly of pressure
Where vertebrae taps skull?

Why won't these debts recede?

The cost of asceticism
Exceeds inflation
While Homeland Security
Lingers misdirected by the empire of greed

Aha, caught again
Spinning my wheels to the melodies
Of network news

How is it possible
For love to hide
Behind a mirage?

Sight and Insight

There are those
Who say this dream is not real

They're wrong

Fathers fret
When toddlers tumble backward

But walking involves patience, skill
Gentle guidance
And stout limbs

If sensible leaders
Cannot feel
The grace infused
In ever-present dreaming
That doesn't mean it isn't bona fide

It means parental guidance
Is disregarded

No cause for panic
Wait
Patiently
Skillfully
In your perfect spot

Healed by Awe

Just a moment ago
My chest welled content
With only surrender

What's it like …humanity?

Moths at midnight
Flying to hallowed light
With or without understanding

Irresistible brightness
Blinding us
To arrogance, imagination and opinion

Burning our bones
But not the story that warms them

Con Artist

This ego is clever
Knowing every scam in the book

Don't be fooled to inaction

Sometimes cruelty is friendship
And demolition, reconstruction

This slippery ego
Loves sentiment
"I'm good. I'm bad."

That's when it knows
You're crippled and confused

Hack off clinging ensnared beliefs
And do not run from war

An infant wails and mother's milk flows freely
Subservient to its blubbering master

Likewise honest love knows no religion
Has little to do with words
And much to do with tears

Gold Mining

Two weeks fasting
Restores inner appetite
For all things natural

Multilayered
Deep earthly oceans
Emerge uncontested
From idle senses

What challenges nature's wines
Seasoned by weeks
Of kindhearted denial?

Nothing

No maiden
Can resist the virility
Born from years of manly abstinence
Its spices
Mysterious brews
And holy manna

Fourteen days fortifies
Brain and belly
Casting ancient choirs
Chanting spontaneous mantras
To angel hums
Eagerly restoring the divinity of souls
To gold in a melting pot

Chrematophobia

I yearn to chant an elegy
A prayer
To the Divinity of assets
Asking her
To remove my fear
My affliction
The one that
Keeps me poor and false

But I'm afraid
Of seeds I've sown

Weary of selling my time
For food, protection and comfort
My stomach chokes
From the evidence of my own denial

Why am I eclipsed
By fiscal emaciation?
A mother will walk on water
To spare her child

This is my design

Drowning in holy water
Arms outstretched
Reaching up
Unafraid
Of false invention

My mother taught me
The wisdom of Deutschland
"Don't waste breath on failure …work"

Swallow fear
Allow sensation
Travel
Write
Honor truthful coffeehouses
Eunoia

With or without alms
The goddess of assets
Grants boons to honest motivation

Reaching up undaunted
Trusting
That answered prayers
At hand
Begin inside

New Year's Eve

Old habits
Still heavy
May bind your feet to hardened dung

But you are not weak

A single resolution
Buys back
Your birthright

Every wave
Perfectly timed
Finds its way to shore

I used to suppose
I would die
Without ever being heard

I never imagined
The transcendent scale
Of volumes
Condensed in one verse
One note

When the fog clears
All you can do is weep willingly
And flower a laughing Buddha

Hunting

I saw rifles
And knew …hunters
A faint sent of booze assaulted me

They ogled me like I was a snack

Like a lion
I proclaimed
"I'm a hunter too!"

"Once I hunted women and gold
But now, I hunt good judgment, without a permit
Presently, I'm stalking you"

(It was like having a conversation with eggs)

I invited myself to walk alongside
Discharging photos
To comprehend the moment of inspiration
And witness them hatch

I told a story about my godfather
Hunting Canadian moose
A rack so grand
We played on it like a teeter-totter

One of them threw up

I offered to drive them home
And they agreed

They didn't realize
You catch what you pursue

I later framed the moment
In one hundred twenty-five words
My trophy for good judgment

Word of Mouth News

Casual hearsay is slick like ice
Suitable conventions
Slide anywhere
Don't they?

You tell me you are rich
I see poverty
You tell me you're a lion
I see a fish
You say life's a game
I say checkmate

On this side of the room
I'm a joker
On the other
A poet

Both are right
And wrong

Banter is slippery
Be mindful who you accuse of hallucination

Saga of Halo

Did I really originate from semen?
My father's father's father ...and the rest

Tracing history
From eggs and sperm
Exposes a vulnerable kinship

My very-great-great-grandfather, Adam
Named every animal, with Eve
My very-great-great-grandmother

Subsequently, they ate a rotten apple

Is that why I'm suspicious of apple-selling serpents
To this day?

The illumination you give off
Did that come from frogspawn as well?

Seeing Love

What puts my spirit at ease
Is knowing
That all my unpaid sums
Will be settled justly

What a celebration this brings my mind

This rollercoaster
Of self-seduction
Piercing my addiction
With too sober a demeanor

What cruel irony

Each friend is more handsome
Liberated from debt
And tee-totaled spirit dealers
With fashionable currency

This entire ocean
Of woven words
Is meaningless
When personal fortune
Is hidden from view

In the middle of the night
Reflections of wounded souls
Speak plainly;
You can only look at love
With love

Theodora

Today
This dinner table is alive
With theologians
Experts on the strata of heaven and hell

Some say, heaven is a pen for sheep
Others say, only illumination and love subsists

Apparently, we've run out of honest wine
I'll fetch more

It's all I really care about

Radio Interview

You asked
"What about death?"

Laughing deep bellied
With tears
I counter

"My favorite theme"
"We must talk about useful death
Aren't we tired of sex, money, war and network news?"

Everyone drinks this esoteric nectar

Let's get drunk
And leave denial behind

Whatever road we travel
Death waits
For our surrender

You ask
"Isn't this slavery?"

Deep bellied again
Yielding to delight

"Yes"

Laying down what we love
For what we love more
Is imprisonment

Love gives us no alternative
Iron filings to a magnet
Rapture enslaves us

Knowing this,
If we keep up this interview,
Your listeners may leave themselves behind

We need to chat more on sweet death
Before the wine is gone

Abstract Mariners

Most of my friends are fish
Powerless to be without the ocean

To my surprise
No two are comparable

Except at daybreak
When each opens easily with enthusiastic dreams
And recounts stories
Devoid of fear
Suspicion or withholding

Marine life
Is straight away recognizable

Vast gills
Immovability

Ocean reliance
Betrays their disguise

If that doesn't do it
The mirrors fixed to their foreheads
Confirms authenticity

Iowa Compost

Nature
In its perfection
Recycles everything
Reusing
Every wicked thought
As fertilizer
For new growth

A wise washerwoman
Once told me
"Many in Fairfield
Are apt in self-merit"

Agreeably
This copious crop
Is loaded with organic dung
The soul of its soul
Rich in uncontaminated original seed

Occupation

Formerly, an ancient wild owl
Shot me a glance
(Or was it a stare?)
Overwhelming me
With verse
Too vast and impossible
For my undersized vessel

Thirty years later
Still suckling
(Or is it addiction?)
Scarred wines so fizzy
I am mute
Irrepressible
And fictitious

It's an engaging preoccupation too
Otherwise
I'd just be waiting to leave

Those Asleep May Miss It

In sleep
A secret connection
A remembrance
Escapes

Tugging an umbilical line
Urging my body and soul to meet

We cannot always understand
What nature intends
Lest time, space and energy
Cease to exist or merge

Still
At times
I fear infinity

Don't try to reason it out
Trust the premonition in your gut
By no means ignore this natural gift
Honest directions
Leaked from the Department of Good Judgment

Just listen
Sleep peacefully
And perform

All This

What a fool
I've carried this allowance in my wallet for twenty
years

Do you remember when I asked
"What would you do with eleven million dollars?"
You answered, "This"

Again I inquired after ten years
You answered, "This"

Today, I ask
"This"

For twenty-three years
I've endured the pinch in my pocket
Tempting deposit
But "This" was far more vital

Diet

Is it true?
You are what you eat?

Christians eat blood and flesh
To be Jesus
Eating majesty
They become majestic

What do fanatics eat?
Overcooked scripture?

Fasting forty days
Ingesting nothing
Will you become nothing?

Circus

My marriage
Is a supernatural friendship
Conforming to no known laws of nature

The inscrutable law of friendship
Warms me   .
Like the sun under my skin

Nonetheless
I advocate granting no merit
To the special effects sustained by connubial drama
And its three-ringed circus of erosion

Chicken

Sometimes
The sound of my wife's thoughts
Drive me mad
Thought following thought
Pecking and scratching loose threads
And shiny objects

Listen
Don't talk
She longs for irresistible affection
At the bottom of the well

Harvard Grad

Does greed bewitch you?
How you gain prosperity
Merits more than motivations

Never trust a man who says
"It's only business"

Your gurus
Teaching false integrity
Ought to remain in school
And polish the future

Pay attention
This moment is all there is
Soon we will leave
And the earth will be without its darlings

Genesis

In the beginning
God was a poet
With one word

Sailors' Voyage

Somewhere
Memories
Loud
With immeasurable means and sacred libraries
Assail me

Love
Dissolving princely verve
Urges me to reside beneath this tree

But what a tree!

Now I am a servant, in servants' quarters
With three masters
Who are kingdoms to me

This is what love does
It tips every boat

Institution

Only God knows
Who God is

A few inhabitants
Imitating mystic habits
Have cultured pop idols
Composing inspired songs
Devoid of royal belts and thrones

Scriptures were compiled
Granting mutual equality
Liberty and confinement
For Holy Spirits
The Board of Directors
And their management teams

Caveat emptor

The music of your own soul
Remedies all deficiencies

Children

There is laughter hidden in my chest
Wresting with compassion

Wrangling together in amorous grips
You were born

This puzzle survives everywhere
Enriching the colors of the world

Rain water flooding
In chorus
Through all rivers at once

Little Margins

This drum keeps pounding in my head
Words aren't saying what I feel
Small sounds, heaped like bricks, build higher walls
Shaping drawn-out mazes

Naked, I see you naked
But each verse covers your busting breasts
Hiding what must never be hidden
For fear that all mankind will be rendered impotent

This soul is so precious
Please don't mistake me for the corpse I clothe

Once

I don't remember what I once was
A baby seeking toys perhaps

This search for games of sex and war, love and wisdom
Stopped when you showed me this mirror

And all that I imagined
Was indistinguishable from you

Coliseum

More trouble in the world
CNN tells me

Viewers worshiping difficulties
Coveting great heroes
Invoking great adversaries

Supersized sex
Women mounting men
Recapturing maternal spirit

Two hundred million subscribers
Craving pain
And the hope of escape

I know Anderson is keeping us honest
But the real news is
There is no news

Just this precious breath
And its poetry

Emo Traffic

Study resistance
It points
To daybreak

Just turn around and see it

Loyal Practitioner

So many people
Want to lock me away
And who can blame them
Sometimes
I believe the same

After all
I've been digging this well for forty years
Water is flooding everything
But I am parched
And now my skin is itchy

When I told you I drank the starry firmament
I wasn't kidding
But that doesn't mean
The cows treat me special
They still poop on my shoes

About the Author

Rodney Charles

(Saskatchewan Borealis)

I was young
When the never failing flame of Queen City's oil
refinery
Blazed both eerie and calming
At once

Like losing individuality

I never imagined
One day
The open sky would consume every memory
Changing crude to gasoline

Like the gravity of love

My close friends tell me
I've spent too many Canadian winters
Freezing neurons

They're right
And that's how I know
They're honest souls

But my own wolf pack
Saskatchewan bred
Discovered new verses
Remembering the kindred love
Piercing our bodies supine
The night we lay
Hand in hand
Vulnerable and exposed
Eyes to the stars
Bathed in aurora

And that first kiss
From which I've never recovered